Too much, too soon
The government's plans for your child's sex education

Norman Wells

FAMILY EDUCATION TRUST

FAMILY EDUCATION TRUST
First published 2009

© Family Education Trust, 2009
ISBN (13) 978-0-906229-21-7

Family Education Trust
Jubilee House
19-21 High Street
Whitton
Twickenham
TW2 7LB
email: info@famyouth.org.uk
website: www.famyouth.org.uk

Family Education Trust is a company limited by guarantee
(No 3503533) and a registered charity (No 1070500).

Printed in Great Britain by CW Print Group, Loughton, Essex

Contents

Introduction

In a letter to the *Daily Mail*, 14-year-old Josie Parkinson described the sex education she had been receiving at her local secondary school:

> As a 14 year-old girl, I have had to attend four talks in the past nine months from a woman from a family planning clinic.

> I have been taught three times how to put on a condom; how easily pupils can acquire condoms free at a clinic; how to recognise sexually transmitted diseases and have them treated confidentially at a clinic; and that we do not need to tell our parents, GP, the police or anyone else in authority about being provided with contraception, or even having an abortion.

> There was not one mention of abstaining or any discouragement of sex. At the first lesson we were told: 'As you know, it is unlawful for a girl or boy to have sex before 16. However, if you are under 16, we can still provide you with contraception and you do not need to tell your parents about it.'[1]

There are few parts of the school curriculum which have been surrounded by greater controversy and aroused stronger feelings over the past 30-40 years than sex education. Amid growing concern about high teenage conception rates and escalating rates of sexually transmitted infections among young people, the argument has been repeatedly made that the answer lies in providing 'quality sex and relationship education' to every child in every school. We are told that the current provision is 'too little, too late, and too biological' and that it is 'patchy' across the country.

Schools have found themselves under pressure from the sex education lobby and from central and local government departments to be seen to be playing their part in addressing the social ills that have arisen as a result of the sexual revolution. Yet at the same time they have been conscious of the fact that many parents are by no means convinced that sex education is the answer and that many parents are distinctly uncomfortable about

---

[1] *Daily Mail*, 27 October 2006.

classroom teaching on sexual practices and contraception. Many schools have also been wary of attracting the attention of the local and national press and so have adopted a more cautious approach than sex education campaigners would wish.

Mindful of the restraining effect of 'the two Ps' – parents and the press – the sex education lobby has insisted that the government must take the lead. Only by making sex and relationship education a statutory part of the national curriculum would it be possible to ensure that every child receives his or her 'entitlement' to sex education of a consistently high standard. That way schools would have nothing to fear from parents. If any parent objected to what was on offer, the school could hide behind the law and say it had no choice; it was simply obeying government orders. As for the media, if every school were subject to the same curriculum requirements, no headteacher need fear of being singled out for public exposure.

But what of parents? All too often they have been left confused, bewildered and with a sense of disempowerment:

• What do schools have to teach about sex and relationships?
• Is it compulsory or not?
• At what age does it have to begin?
• Do I have any influence over what my child is taught?
• Is it possible for me to remove my child from sex education classes?
• Is there any proof that sex education will reduce teenage pregnancy and sexually transmitted infection rates?
• Is it true that the Netherlands has much lower teenage pregancy rates because sex education there is more explicit and starts earlier?
• Will I be harming my child if I tell him or her that sex outside marriage is wrong?

It is in order to answer these and other questions that this booklet has been written.

In the following pages we shall show that behind plausible-sounding arguments and innocuous-sounding words there is a specific agenda at work to undermine the role of parents and to tear down traditional moral standards. Sex education is an ideological battlefield on which a war is being waged for the hearts and minds of our children. It is a fast-moving scene. The need for parents to be alert and vigilant has never been greater.

1. The current state of play

The law states that schools must provide a balanced and broadly-based curriculum which:

(a) promotes the spiritual, moral, cultural, mental and physical development of pupils at the school and of society and

(b) prepares such pupils for the opportunities, responsibilities and experiences of adult life.[1]

All maintained schools are required to produce a written statement of their policy with regard to the provision of sex education. They are also required to 'make copies of the statement available for inspection (at all reasonable times) by parents of registered pupils at the school and provide a copy of the statement free of charge to any such parent who asks for one'.[2]

In the case of **primary schools**, there is no requirement to provide sex education. The policy may simply state that no sex education is given beyond aspects of reproduction covered in the science curriculum.

Secondary schools, however, are required to provide sex education for all registered pupils at the school, including education about AIDS and HIV and any other sexually transmitted disease.[3] However, these specific areas, together with aspects of human sexual behaviour other than biological aspects may not be taught as part of national curriculum science, but must be treated as a separate subject.[4]

Local authorities, governing bodies and headteachers are required to ensure that sex education is given 'in such a manner as to encourage those pupils to have due regard to moral considerations and the value of family life'.[5] In addition, headteachers and school governors must have regard to government guidance intended to ensure that children:

---

[1] Education Act 1996, s351.
[2] Education Act 1996, s404.
[3] Education Act 1996, s352.
[4] Education Act 1996, s356(9).
[5] Education Act 1996, s403.

(a) learn the nature of marriage and its importance for family life and the bringing up of children, and

(b) are protected from teaching and materials which are inappropriate having regard to the age and the religious and cultural background of the pupils concerned.[6]

Parents have the legal right to withdraw their children from all or any part of sex education provision. A statement to this effect must be included within the school's policy statement. Parents are not, however, entitled to remove their children from any areas covered by the national curriculum.[7]

Sex and Relationship Education Guidance

In July 2000, the government issued new guidance which stressed that sex and relationship education (SRE) should be firmly rooted in the broader framework for Personal, Social and Health Education (PSHE).[8]

Although primary legislation insisted on the importance of children learning 'the nature of marriage and its importance for family life and the bringing up of children', the guidance is far more ambivalent about its support for marriage. It states that:

[T]he Government recognises…that there are strong and mutually supportive relationships outside marriage. Therefore pupils should learn the significance of marriage and stable relationships as key building blocks of community and society.[9]

The guidance contains a strong emphasis on the need for schools to consult with parents on their sex education policies. In a chapter devoted to 'Working with Parents', the guidance recognises that:

Parents are the key people in:

• teaching their children about sex and relationships;

• maintaining the culture and ethos of the family;

[6] Education Act 1996, s403, as amended by the Learning and Skills Act 2000, s148.

[7] Education Act 1996, s405.

[8] PSHE now stands for Personal, Social, Health and Economic education and currently consists of: nutrition and physical activity, drugs, alcohol and tobacco education, sex and relationships education, emotional health and wellbeing, safety, careers education, work-related learning, and personal finance.

[9] Department for Education and Employment, Sex and Relationship Education Guidance, July 2000, Ref 0116/2000, para 4.

- helping their children cope with the emotional and physical aspects of growing up; and
- preparing them for the challenges and responsibilities that sexual maturity brings.[10]

Programmes of study

In 2007 the Qualifications and Curriculum Authority (QCA) published new non-statutory programmes of study for PSHE education at key stages 3 and 4, which came into effect from September 2008. At key stages 3 and 4, PSHE has been split into two:

- economic wellbeing and financial capability, consisting of careers education, work-related learning, enterprise, and financial capability; and
- personal wellbeing, concentrating on the personal development of pupils and covering sex and relationships, as well as drugs education.[11]

These documents are framed in very broad terms and are capable of a wide range of interpretations, but the general tone indicates that there is no recognition of moral absolutes and that young people are not to be given any clear moral direction. For example, the programme of study for personal wellbeing at key stage 3 (11-14 year-olds) refers to the need for pupils to 'clarify their own values' – a phrase which means that there is no such thing as objective right and wrong, but that pupils must decide what is right 'for them'. It also states that children should learn about 'the nature and importance of marriage and of stable relationships for family life and bringing up children', as if there were no difference between marriage and unmarried partnerships. The programme of study makes several references to the need to teach 11-14 year-olds about sexual orientation, same-sex relationships and civil partnerships and recommends the *fpa* and Brook as sources of help.

The programme of study for personal wellbeing at key stage 4 (14-16 year-olds) covers similar ground and recommends that opportunities are taken 'to review and build upon earlier learning about contraception, sexually transmitted infections and HIV'. It also appears to equate

---

[10] *ibid.*, para 5.3.

[11] The relevant documents for Key Stage 3 can be accessed at *http://www.qca.org.uk/libraryAssets/media/PSHE-pers-ks3.pdf* and *http://www.qca.org.uk/libraryAssets/media/PSHE-econ-ks3.pdf* The documents for Key Stage 4 are available at *http://www.qca.org.uk/libraryAssets/media/PSHE-pers-ks4.pdf* and *http://www.qca.org. uk/libraryAssets/media/PSHE-econ-ks4.pdf*

marriage with same-sex civil partnerships and to assume that both types of relationship are of equal benefit and stability when it states that: 'Students should address the role and benefits of marriage and civil partnerships in stable relationships and family life, building on key stage 3 learning.'

2. The sex educators' agenda

The *fpa* (formerly the Family Planning Association) and Brook are two of the key players in the campaign for more sex education beginning at an earlier age. Both organisations are represented on the government's independent advisory groups on sexual health and teenage pregnancy, and both played a key role in the government's review of sex education delivery in schools during 2008. They are also prominent members of the Sex Education Forum, a government-funded umbrella organisation consisting of 50 groups, which claims to be 'the national authority on Sex and Relationships Education'.

In this chapter, we shall draw on publications and statements made by the *fpa* and Brook in order to identify precisely what they hope sex and relationship education will achieve.

Encouraging sexual experimentation

The Brook leaflets *Do you come here often?* and *Whatever turns you on* seek to 'encourage young people to see giving and receiving sexual pleasure in terms other than penetrative sex' and 'inform young people about how this can be achieved'.[1] In response to the question, 'I know she likes me, but how do I find out how far she'll go?' Brook's highly controversial magazine-style guide *Say Yes? Say No? Say Maybe?* advises boys to ask:

> I'd like to kiss you – to touch your breasts – to put my hand on your leg – is that OK? Can I stroke you here – do you like that? Am I hurting you? Is this nice for you?

It goes onto say:

> [O]nce you get the knack, it *does* make it easier to get along with people – and get off with them too. All you have to do is open your mouth, *ask* what they want, and *say* what you want – try it![2]

---

[1] Brook, *Making sex education easier: A guide to sex education and sex education resources from Brook Publications.*
[2] Suzie Hayman, *Say 'Yes'? Say 'No'? Say 'Maybe'?* Brook, 1999.

There is a passing reference to the age of consent towards the end of the publication, but it continues to talk about 'boys' and 'girls' obtaining contraception to 'go the whole distance' and show 'how *really* grown-up and loving' they are. The over-riding message is summed up in the closing punchline: 'You can loveplay, foreplay, any kind of sexplay…but best of all, playsafe.'[3]

In her introduction to the the *Sex Education Source Book*, Doreen Massey, former director of the *fpa* and current chair of the All-Party Parliamentary Group for Children, writes that the purpose of sex education is to teach children 'to express love without embarrassment, and to find and give pleasure in sexual encounters when it is appropriate'. She omits to specify, however, when such sexual encounters are 'appropriate', leaving it entirely down to pupils to make that decision for themselves.[4]

Advancing relativism

According to the sex education establishment there are no moral absolutes when it comes to sexual activity. In the words of an *fpa* leaflet for young people, 'What's right for YOU is what's important here.'[5] The position is explained more fully in another *fpa* publication:

> How do you know you love someone? When is it right to have sex? How do you know you are ready? When are you ready to have children? How can you be sure marriage is right for you or not? Should you only have one partner at a time? These questions that have been dilemmas over many generations are increased by the modern pressures on young people to be as adventurous and accumulative in their sexual lives as they are expected to be in their material lives.

> Few of us can offer simple answers to young people – yes or no, this is right or wrong. Our task is to assist the young to find their way through life's minefields as confidently, positively and unharmed as possible.[6]

Marriage does not feature very prominently at all in guides produced by organisations which have the ear of the government with regard to sex education. Indeed, the fpa *Primary School Workbook* discourages teachers from making too much of marriage:

---

[3] *ibid.*

[4] Doreen E Massey (ed), *Sex Education Source Book: Current issues and debates*, fpa, 1995, p.7.

[5] *Is everybody doing it? Your guide to contraception*, fpa, 2000.

[6] *Sex Education Source Book*, op. cit., p.44.

Rather than discussing relationships within the context of marriage, talk about commitment and the specialness of a sexual relationship.[7]

Breaking down traditional moral standards

The *fpa*'s practical guide to developing sex education in schools suggests that adherence to a strict moral code places children at a distinct disadvantage in life. It is therefore the task of sex education to broaden children's horizons and present them with options beyond the confines of their parents' limited vision:

> It can be difficult for parents who strongly adhere to a distinct moral code to prepare their child for the variety of attitudes towards relationships and sexuality which different faiths, cultures and ethnic groups hold within our society. A balanced programme of sex education in school gives children and young people the opportunity to learn about the whole human experience of sexuality. They are able to examine their own values and beliefs in the light of those held by others, to separate fact from fiction, to recognise and to refuse to tolerate prejudice, and to learn to respect diversity. Deeper understanding of the values and beliefs that they hold can help young people to clarify why they think and behave as they do and increases the options available to them, enabling them to make informed decisions.[8]

The *Sex Education Source Book* makes a similar point more succinctly:

> Promoting any one lifestyle to young people is not good practice. Children need to develop an understanding of diversity of lifestyles... [A]n enriching understanding can be developed through accepting and celebrating difference.[9]

In a later chapter, the source book suggests that a liberal approach to sex education is superior to an approach based on a firm moral code:

> If anything, a liberal, humanistic approach to the topic is likely to be more value-rich in that it will seek to explore a number of different values and beliefs.[10]

---

[7] Gill Lenderyou, *The Primary School Workbook*, fpa, 1994, p.71.
[8] Gill Mullinar, *Developing sex education in schools: a practical guide*, fpa, 1994, p.13.
[9] *Sex Education Source Book*, op. cit., p.54.
[10] *ibid.*, p.87.

Promoting homosexuality as normal and natural

The *fpa* encourages teachers to positively celebrate 'different sexualities':

> It is...important to encourage discussion of homosexuality amongst those young people who are not lesbian or gay. If we seek to promote sexual health, then we must address the myths and prejudices surrounding sexual orientation and encourage not merely acceptance or tolerance but celebration of different sexualities.[11]

In an effort to foster a climate within the classroom which values a diversity of beliefs, the same publication later encourages schools to explore homosexuality in relation to the humanities, history, the arts, literature etc.[12]

Redefining the family

According to the *fpa*'s practical guide to developing sex education in schools, 'schools need to interpret the word "family" in a way which includes everyone and avoids damaging any pupil's sense of self-worth'. The guide goes on to commend the World Health Organisation's definition of the family:

> Our concept of family is not limited to relationships of blood, marriage, sexual partnership or adoption. It extends to a broad range of groups whose bonds are based on feelings of trust, mutual support and a shared destiny.[13]

In fact, nothing appears to be off-limits for the sex education lobby. So much so that the *fpa* can warmly commend a book that took a non-judgmental approach to bestiality and all manner of other sexual practices most parents would not even think of discussing as a matter of routine with their children. Twenty-six years after the publication of *Make it Happy: What sex is all about*, the *fpa*'s communications officer could write: 'The book remains a testament to what good literature on sex education should be.'[14]

---

[11] *ibid.*, p.12.

[12] *ibid.*, p.85.

[13] *Developing sex education in schools*, op. cit., p.40.

[14] Review of 'Make it Happy: What sex is all about', *Young People Now*, 10-16 March 2004.

3. The campaign for statutory sex education

It has been a longstanding objective of sex education campaigners to raise the status of their subject by making it a statutory part of the national curriculum. They have strongly objected to the current arrangement whereby schools are required to have regard to the wishes of parents when determining their policies and parents are entitled to withdraw their children from sex education classes. A practical guide to developing sex education in schools published by the *fpa* asserted: 'sex education is an equal opportunities issue – all children and young people are entitled to it'.[1]

The children's rights lobby has also been vociferous in its demand that parents should not be able to deprive their children of their 'right to know' in the area of sexuality and sexual practice. For example, in 1994, the Children's Rights Development Unit was 'disturbed' by the thought of parents being able to control and veto the sex education received by their children. In its *UK Agenda for Children*, it asserted that:

> [S]ex education in school, linked to the National Curriculum, should be available to all children and young people, and taught at an age when it will be of use to them and in a manner sensitive to their needs. Governors should not be responsible for deciding whether or not a school provides sex education. There should be special training for staff involved and parents should not have the right to withdraw their children.[2]

In 2006 the UK Youth Parliament launched a national campaign on sex and relationship education. The following summer, it published a report that concluded:

- SRE should be an entitlement for all children and young people and taught as part of statutory provision of PSHE.
- Parents should not be able to make the decision to withdraw their child from SRE.

[1] Gill Mullinar, *Developing sex education in schools: a practical guide*, fpa, 1994, p12.
[2] Gerison Lansdown and Peter Newell, *UK agenda for children*. London: CRDU, 1994, p106.

- No school should be able to opt out of delivering good SRE to their pupils and this includes primary schools, faith schools and academies.
- SRE needs to be taught throughout a pupil's time in education.[3]

In December 2007, the campaign for statutory SRE was given fresh impetus by the announcement in the Children's Plan that the government would 'review best practice in effective sex and relationships education and how it is delivered in schools'.[4] Labour MP, Chris Bryant, was among the first in the queue to press for statutory SRE,[5] and as the year wore on, it was clear that we were in the grip of a concerted campaign.

In all their public statements, government ministers resolutely refused to entertain the prospect of making PSHE, including SRE, a statutory part of the national curriculum.

- The schools minister Jim Knight said: 'Ofsted has told us that too much time and effort have been spent discussing whether PSHE should be a statutory subject. Making something statutory does not ensure that it is provided effectively—or, indeed, at all.'[6]
- In its response to the Teenage Pregnancy Independent Advisory Group in February 2008, the government dismissed calls to put PSHE on a statutory footing on the basis that Parliament had relatively recently decided against such a move during the passage of the Education and Inspections Bill in 2006.[7]
- Lord Adonis was quite clear that the future position of PSHE within the curriculum would not be revisited until the government had considered the primary curriculum review, together with the reviews of drugs education and sex and relationships education.[8]

However, this did not dampen the enthusiasm of the campaigners and over the summer months, scarcely a week went by without renewed calls from one group or another demanding compulsory sex education for all children from the very beginning of primary school. The following examples are taken almost at random:

[3] UK Youth Parliament, *Are You Getting It?* June 2007.
[4] Department for Children, Schools and Families, *The Children's Plan,* December 2007, p13.
[5] Chris Bryant, *Teenage Mums,* January 2008.
[6] HC Hansard, 17 December 2007, cols 584-585.
[7] Government Response to the 4th Annual Report of the Teenage Pregnancy Independent Advisory Group.
[8] HL Hansard, 21 July 2008, col 1552.

- In early July 2008, the *fpa* and Brook attracted prominent press and media coverage without even so much as a press release.[9]
- Delegates at the British Medical Association conference supported a motion calling for mandatory sex education for all school children, delivered by specialist teachers 'to a nationally standardised curriculum', incorporating contraception and 'how it may be accessed', beginning 'at primary school entry'.
- The Teenage Pregnancy Independent Advisory Group (TPIAG) published a report recommending compulsory sex education in all schools and revised government guidance that was explicit in stating what should be taught and learnt at each key stage. TPIAG also called for a clear statement that all schools, including faith schools, must teach all aspects of SRE in an anti-discriminatory way. Since contraception, abortion and homosexuality were all legal, all children and young people should be able to learn about them. The group also demanded the removal of any restriction on advertising condoms on television before the watershed.[10]
- This was followed by a call from the Independent Advisory Group on Sexual Health and HIV to make PSHE and all elements of SRE a statutory subject at all key stages.[11]
- The House of Lords debated an amendment to the Education and Skills Bill aimed at making PSHE, incorporating sex education, a statutory part of the curriculum, though it did not proceed to a vote.[12]
- In August, a cross-party group of MPs, together with leading sex education advocate Gill Frances and the chief executive of the UK Youth Parliament wrote a letter to the *Daily Telegraph* calling for compulsory sex education for all children.[13]
- BBC Radio 5 Live launched an online sex education questionnaire which was loaded with so many presuppositions that it was almost impossible to respond to.

[9] See, for example, Anthea Lipsett, 'Give four-year-olds sex education, say charities', *Guardian,* 4 July 2008; Sarah Harris, 'Sex lessons for children age 4', *Daily Mail,* 5 July 2008.

[10] Teenage Pregnancy Independent Advisory Group, *Annual Report 2007/08.*

[11] *Progress and priorities – working together for high quality sexual health: Review of the National Strategy for Sexual Health and HIV,* produced for the Independent Advisory Group on Sexual Health and HIV by the Medical Foundation for AIDS and Sexual Health, July 2008.

[12] HL Hansard, 21 July 2008, cols 1546-1553.

[13] *Daily Telegraph,* 26 August 2008.

- Channel 4 launched a six-part *Sex Education Show* containing explicit sexual content, shown before the watershed.
- The *fpa* ensured that primary school sex education remained in the news by releasing a comic for six year-olds designed to teach them the names of intimate body parts.[14]

When the government had launched the promised review of sex and relationship education delivery in February 2008, a consideration of the status of PSHE lay outside its remit. Nevertheless, when the steering group published its report in October 2008, it carried a strong recommendation to make PSHE a statutory part of the national curriculum.[15] Given the make-up of the government-appointed group, this came as no surprise. The 25-strong steering group included three members of the UK Youth Parliament, together with representatives from the Sex Education Forum, Brook, the Terrence Higgins Trust, and the *fpa*. The chair of the Teenage Pregnancy Independent Advisory Group, Gill Frances, was also involved, as was Professor Roger Ingham who has long been an advocate of earlier sex education.

What is alarming, however, is the government's readiness to support such a far-reaching recommendation without any public consultation. In addition to the public pronouncements made by ministers in the course of the year, the schools minister Jim Knight had given pro-family groups an assurance that there would be a full public consultation on any substantive recommendations made by the review group before any decisions were taken.

Independent review of PSHE

In its response to the steering group's report, the government announced the establishment of an independent review chaired by London headmaster, Sir Alasdair Macdonald, to consider 'the most effective ways of making PSHE statutory' and 'the best ways to provide a statutory entitlement to PSHE education for all pupils'. Sir Alasdair's review got under way very quietly in mid-November when 80 'key stakeholders' received an email from the Department for Children, Schools and Families (DCSF)

[14] *Let's grow with Nisha and Joe*, fpa, 2008.
[15] Review of Sex and Relationship Education (SRE) in Schools, A report by the External Steering Group, October 2008.

inviting their input. Stakeholders were given just three weeks to respond to 11 questions, including:

- What are the best ways to balance a statutory entitlement to PSHE education with sufficient flexibility for individual schools?

- How can the rights of parents to withdraw their children from parts of sex and relationships education be balanced with the rights of young people to have access to PSHE provision that meets their needs?

- Given the current demands of the curriculum, how can statutory PSHE education best be accommodated?

- What are the major barriers to successful implementation of statutory PSHE education, and how might these be overcome?

- What scope is there for extra-curricular activity to contribute to PSHE education?

When Sir Alasdair Macdonald's report was published at the end of April 2009, it supported the government's intention to make PSHE a statutory part of the national curriculum. However, given that his review was predicated on the assumption that PSHE would be made statutory, he was hardly at liberty to conclude otherwise. Nevertheless, the government has welcomed the report with open arms, presenting it as a ringing endorsement of its proposals.[16]

Holding the government to account

Given the government's clear written commitment to consult on any substantive recommendations made by the review group before accepting them, Family Education Trust has pressed ministers to be true to their word.

Initially we were advised by officials that Jim Knight had simply 'forgotten' the commitment to consult. Then we were told that he had made the commitment in good faith, but had not at that time appreciated the strength with which the review group would recommend making PSHE statutory.

Towards the end of 2008, Sarah McCarthy-Fry took over responsibilty for PSHE from Jim Knight. In her view, the government's commitment

---

[16] Department for Children, Schools and Families press release, 'Macdonald: Personal, Social, Health and Economic Education should be compulsory', Press Notice 2009/0078, 28 April 2008; HC Hansard, 27 Apr 2009, cols 31-32WS.

to consult on the content of PSHE but not on whether it should be made statutory was 'very much in line with the spirit of commitments' made earlier in the year. However, when we pointed out that what the minister was saying was in line neither with the letter nor the spirit of earlier written commitments but was rather diametrically opposed to previous undertakings, she finally agreed that the government's intention to give PSHE statutory status would be subject to public consultation.[17]

[17] The resultant consultation was launched on 30 April 2009 under the management of the Qualifications and Curriculum Authority - *http://www.qca.org.uk/qca_22258.aspx*

4. What is wrong with making sex education statutory?

The government's intention to make PSHE, including sex and relationship education, a statutory part of the curriculum is a cause of concern for several reasons:

It would limit the influence of parents

Making PSHE statutory would inevitably reduce the influence of parents over what is taught. Schools are currently required to consult with parents with regard to their sex education policies and to be sensitive to their wishes with regard to what is taught. However, making PSHE part of the national curriculum would inevitably make schools less accountable to parents in what is a particularly sensitive and controversial subject area.

Genito-urinary medicine consultant and sex education campaigner, Colm O'Mahony, has expressed the view that:

> To improve sex and relationship education, legislation is needed to make it a statutory duty for schools to teach it competently. I think schools will probably even like this, because then parents can be told that this has to be done and the risk of parental complaints is greatly reduced.[1]

It would limit the discretion of individual schools

At the moment, schools are free to develop their own policies on sex education in line with their own ethos. However, to mandate PSHE centrally would inevitably remove discretion from schools at the local level, to a greater or lesser extent. One of the government's stated aims in proposing to make PSHE statutory is to ensure consistency. This raises the very real possibility that some schools would be forced to compromise their beliefs on controversial areas such as contraception, abortion and homosexuality in the name of consistency. Allowing schools flexibility

[1] Davina McCall and Anita Naik, *Let's Talk Sex*, Channel 4, 2007, p.13.

to teach sex education in line with their ethical and moral values is incompatible with the goal of consistency.

It would deprive primary schools of any choice in the matter

While primary schools are currently required to have a policy on sex education, they are under no obligation to teach anything beyond the requirements of national curriculum science. However, if PSHE were to be made statutory at all key stages, the governing bodies and headteachers of primary schools would have no option but to provide sex education.

It would run counter to general education policy

There are already considerable pressures on the curriculum, and making PSHE statutory seems to run contrary to the government's general policy on education. Government minister, Sarah McCarthy-Fry has stated: 'Recent curriculum developments have been aimed at reducing the statutory core and allowing schools even more autonomy to organise their curriculum.'[2] However, making PSHE statutory would be a step in the opposite direction.

There is a lack of firm evidence for the effectiveness of sex education

It is not even as if there is any evidence to demonstrate that statutory SRE will have any positive effect. In fact, there is not even any consensus as to what constitutes effectiveness (see chapter 5, 'Is there any evidence that sex education works?').

Parents would be inclined to take less responsibility for their children

Most of the components of PSHE are the primary responsibility of parents; for example, nutrition and physical activity, drugs, alcohol and tobacco education, sex and relationships education, emotional health and well-being, safety, and personal finance. There is no question that the

---

[2] HC Hansard, 3 Nov 2008, Col 185W.

more that schools take responsibility to themselves for these areas, the less that parents will see them as their responsibility.

If PSHE were to become a statutory part of the curriculum alongside other curriculum subjects, there would be a very real danger that parents would no more consider themselves responsible for these aspects of their children's physical, emotional and social development than they typically regard themselves as responsible for the teaching of English, maths, history and science.

If we are serious about encouraging parents to take more, and not less, responsibility for their children, the state, through its schools and other agencies, needs to take care not to undermine them by assuming a parental role.

5. Is there any evidence that sex education works?

Extravagant claims are made for sex and relationship education. According to the Department for Children, Schools and Families:

> The delivery of good SRE is crucial in keeping young people safe and healthy as well as helping to bring down teenage pregnancy rates…

> We know that many young people feel they are not getting sex and relationship education which provides them with the knowledge and skills they need to make safe and well-informed choices, and delay sex until they are ready.

> Evidence shows that quality SRE has a direct impact on reducing teenage pregnancy rates and is an essential strand of the government's teenage pregnancy strategy.[1]

In making his announcement that SRE is to become compulsory in schools from the age of five, Jim Knight, the Schools Minister, asserted that it would help to reduce rates of teenage pregnancy and sexually transmitted infection.[2]

The past three decades have witnessed a substantial increase in the provision of SRE in both primary and secondary schools and it has never been easier for teenagers to obtain contraception without their parents knowing, yet the UK still has the highest rate of teenage conceptions in Western Europe, and sexually transmitted infection rates have continued to rise. An examination of an 'enhanced sex education programme' found that while the programme increased young people's knowledge it had no discernable effect on sexual activity.[3] There is no evidence that starting sex education in primary school would produce results that secondary school sex education has failed to deliver.

---

[1] Department for Children, Schools and Families, 'Review of Sex and Relationship Education Delivery', Press Notice 2008/0029, 25 February 2008.

[2] Department for Children, Schools and Families, *Government Response to the Report by the Sex and Relationship Education (SRE) Review Steering Group,* October 2008, Ministerial Foreword.

[3] M Henderson, 'Impact of a theoretically based sex education programme (SHARE) delivered by teachers on NHS registered conceptions and terminations: final results of cluster randomised trial', *BMJ,* 2007, 334:133.

Written answers to parliamentary questions indicate that the DCSF has not commissioned or evaluated research on the impact of SRE on the attitudes and lifestyle choices of young people;[4] neither has it made any assessment of the effectiveness of SRE.[5] It therefore remains unclear precisely what the Department would regard as 'good SRE' and what it would consider constitutes 'best practice'.

Surprisingly little research has been conducted to evaluate the success of sex education programmes. As the government's own review group noted in its report:

[T]here is a dearth of good quality international evidence on SRE. A literature review of the international evidence that does exist confirms that it is difficult to be precise about the impact of SRE, for a number of reasons. Firstly, there is not always clarity about what the objectives of SRE are. For example, do we judge the success of SRE in terms of reduced unplanned pregnancies and STIs, or through improvements in the quality of sexual and other relationships that young people experience? Second, there is such significant variation in the delivery of SRE that it makes comparisons between programmes difficult.[6]

An editorial in the *British Medical Journal* noted that:

Most studies on sex education programmes in schools examine intermediate outcomes only, such as pupil satisfaction or reported condom use. This often facilitates premature false claims of success, whereas more robust outcome measures such as rates of terminations, unplanned conceptions and STIs show no benefit.[7]

What is the goal of sex education?

One of the governing principles for Sir Alasdair Macdonald's independent review of PSHE was that: 'the quality of teaching and learning needs to improve, better to meet the needs of young people'. But this begs the question of how both 'the quality of teaching and learning' and 'the needs of young people' are to be defined, and who decides. Another of the

[4] HC Hansard, 19 February 2008, col 511W.
[5] HC Hansard, 25 March 2008, col 109W.
[6] Review of Sex and Relationship Education (SRE) in Schools: A report by the External Steering Group, October 2008, para 22.
[7] T Stammers, 'Sexual health in adolescents: "Saved sex" and parental involvement are key to improving outcomes', *BMJ*, 2007, 334:103-4.

governing principles was that: 'Effective provision should lead to improved outcomes for children in terms of knowledge, skills, understanding and behaviour.' But again, what is 'effective provision' and how will it impact the behaviour of young people? Does it mean contraceptive use? Or is it measured in terms of sexual abstinence? If, as a result of statutory sex education, there were a marked increase in the sexual activity of young people, but they all used a condom every time, would that be viewed as a success or a failure?

Sir Alasdair Macdonald's report makes frequent references to 'good practice', 'effective practice', a 'consistently high quality experience of PSHE', the 'underlying aims of PSHE', and PSHE that 'meets pupils' needs', but no attempt is made to define such terms.[8] Yet definition in this area is vitally important.

When the claim is made that abstinence education 'doesn't work' or that contraceptive-based sex education 'does work', it may just be that the person making the assertion has a different idea of what 'working' means and does not regard saving sex for a lifelong marriage to a person of the opposite sex as a desirable objective.

A paper published by the BMA Foundation for AIDS considered that:

> Except in very large studies, it may be unrealistic to expect research to be able to show that school sex education has any directly measurable behavioural or health outcomes, in view of all the other factors which influence sexual health and lifestyles.

With regard to measuring the impact of sex education by 'self-reported age at first intercourse and numbers of partners', the paper stated that while such information would be useful in understanding sexual behaviour, there was 'not a consensus as to whether increasing ages at first intercourse or decreasing numbers of partners are always desirable outcomes'.[9]

Dr Faith Spicer, the founder and director of the London Youth Advisory Centre (now the Brandon Centre) was among those who did not regard increasing levels of sexual activity among young people as an

---

[8] Sir Alasdair Macdonald, Independent Review of the proposal to make Personal, Social, Health and Economic (PSHE) education statutory, April 2009.

[9] BMA Foundation for AIDS, Health Education Authority, Sex Education Forum, 'Using effectiveness research to guide the development of school sex education', BMA Foundation for AIDS, 1997.

undesirable outcome. Addressing a conference on 'The Consequences of Teenage Sexual Activity' organised by Brook, she stated:

> The main task of sex education in the past was to inform the uninformed. Now, I think the main task is to help young people find out what they feel, how they feel and take responsibility for themselves. But it is also doing another very good task. It is breaking away from the idea that sex is dirty, taboo-ridden, bad, into seeing it as something good, valuable and life-enhancing, and that's why I think that sex education can, of course, increase sexual activity, but it isn't necessarily harmful if it does that.[10]

What we should be aiming for

Nineteen-year-old Simon Demetriou provides us with a striking example of the 'new morality' when he writes that,

> [A]s long as you are having sex responsibly, there is no reason that you should be concerned with…peripheral things [like marriage and moral repercussions]… If taught well, 'moral behaviour' should be no more or less than respect and openness for and with your partner.[11]

He pays tribute to his secondary school for sex education lessons that were 'relevant, rational and, best of all, not sanctimonious'. There is little doubt that his teachers communicated their message very clearly and effectively because the attitudes they instilled in him are very much in line with the approach espoused by Brook, the *fpa*, and other sections of the sex education establishment.

In reality, however, it is simply not possible to divorce sexual responsibility from marriage and morality. Mr Demetriou suggests that 'respect and openness for and with your partner' is the only moral framework required; no more, no less. But what kind of respect is involved in engaging in a sexual relationship for 'as long as we feel this way about each other', while running the risk of passing on an STI with possible lifelong consequences?

It is common among sex educators to define the goal of SRE as providing young people with information so that they are empowered

[10] Faith Spicer, 'The Consequences of Teenage Sexual Activity' conference, 27 April 1981.

[11] Simon Demetriou, 'Encouraging young people to think about sex in terms of moral behaviour is harming sex education', *0-19*, 11 July 2005.

to make 'informed choices'. But that is an inadequate and unworthy goal because it allows for young people under the age of consent to make the 'informed choice' of engaging in unlawful intercourse just as much as it allows them to make an 'informed choice' to wait. The advocates of 'informed choice' are setting their sights far too low. It is not 'informed choices' we should be aiming for, but wise, moral and lawful choices, and there is certainly no evidence that the contraceptive-based sex education prevalent in the UK achieves that.

What about the Netherlands?

Advocates for the expansion of sex education frequently hold up the Netherlands as a model. They attribute the comparatively low Dutch teenage pregnancy rates to earlier and more explicit sex education. However, there is no mandatory curriculum or uniform approach to SRE in the Netherlands and in practice delivery varies considerably from school to school, just as it does in the UK. There is no evidence to suggest that low teenage conception rates in the Netherlands are attributable to SRE in Dutch schools.[12]

A more convincing explanation for the lower rates of teenage pregnancy is to be found in the far more traditional patterns of family life found in the Netherlands. Compared with the UK, the Netherlands has a far lower proportion of lone-parent families, out-of-wedlock births, divorces, and mothers in full-time employment. It also provides teenage mothers with lower welfare benefits, and a stigma continues to be attached to teenage pregnancy.[13]

---

[12] Joost van Loon, *Deconstructing the Dutch Utopia*, Family Education Trust, 2003.
http://www.famyouth.org.uk/pdfs/DDU.pdf
[13] ibid., see also *Lessons in Dutch Mythology*, Family Education Trust, 2003.
http://www.famyouth.org.uk/pdfs/LDM.pdf

6. What about sex education in primary schools?

The sex education lobby has sought to allay parental concerns about the proposal to introduce SRE in primary schools by saying that at key stage 1 (ages 5-7), it would amount to little more than teaching children the names for parts of the body. However, given that all parents talk to their children about their bodies when they wash and dress them from their earliest days and are well able to decide whether to use the proper biological terms or other names for their private parts, there is no compelling reason to make such teaching mandatory. It is unconvincing to say the least to advance the view that young people are placed at risk of teenage pregnancy and sexually transmitted infections for want of knowing the proper names for two or three parts of their anatomy from the age of five.

It is equally spurious to defend compulsory sex education on the basis that young children need to learn that their relationship with their parents is different from their relationship with their grandparents, which in turn is different from their relationship to their siblings, their friends, their neighbours and their teachers. Children already learn about different types of relationships in the context of everyday life. There is no need to formalise and professionalise such things by adding them to an already overloaded curriculum.

Given that the government has accepted the external steering group's insistence that 'acceptance of diversity' should form a key part of a 'clear and explicit values framework' for the teaching of SRE,[1] it is almost certain that homosexuality will be presented as a normal and natural lifestyle choice in the context of talking to even very young children about different types of relationship. Such an approach to primary school sex education would certainly have the support of the Sex Education Forum:

---

[1] Department for Children, Schools and Families, *Government Response to the Report by the Sex and Relationship Education (SRE) Review Steering Group*, October 2008.

Respect for diversity...means that SRE must meet the needs of children whatever their family circumstances, abilities or sexuality. SRE needs to reflect the realities of children's very different lives. This will include children...looked after by...same-sex parents. Children need to see these family groupings represented and affirmed within the SRE curriculum and resources.[2]

Introducing sex education at an early age runs the risk of breaking down children's natural sense of reserve. Far from being a hindrance, children's natural inhibitions and sense of modesty in talking about sexual matters are healthy and provide a necessary safeguard against both sexual abuse and casual attitudes towards sexual intimacy later on.

What parents think about sex education in primary schools

"I am appalled that sex education is to be made compulsory in primary schools. The school that my five year-old son attends has a prominent Muslim population and I think they will be most unhappy about this.

"My husband and I will be forced to withdraw our son, and two subsequent children who will be joining the school soon, from sex education. Since, however, such lessons may lead to inappropriate talk in the playground, and since we are also unhappy about having to have our child singled out, and the difficulty of explaining to him why he is being taken out of lessons when he is so young may mean that our only option will be homeschooling. Since I have health problems this will be very difficult for me. I hope there is still time for the government to reconsider."

Mother of three children, Middlesex

---

[2] Caroline Ray and Janine Jolly, *Sex and relationships education for primary age children*, Sex Education Forum, 2002.

"Parents are the ones who have to pick up the pieces when children are exposed at school, without parental knowledge or consent, to material and information which disturbs them, often in a way they are unable to articulate. This applies especially to primary age children. Any attempt to expose them to direct information on the intimate details of human relationships in a public setting, i.e. in a classroom, is unacceptable.

"We believe that intercourse should be reserved solely within the context of marriage. Thus we endeavour to bring up our children with those values, respecting the virtues of chastity, modesty and self-control; never to treat another person as an object for personal pleasure, nor to let themselves be used in that way."

Parents of two children, London

"As a 27 year-old parent with a child approaching primary school age and another on the way, I am horrified that the government could even contemplate that children as young as four or five should need to know about sex education and relationships. What planet are they on? A child under the age of 10 really has no need to know anything of a sexual nature."

Mother of one child, Berkshire

"I am a mother of three children, two of whom attend a primary school intent on delivering the Channel 4 *Living and Growing* programme. Having seen the sexually explicit content of this programme, I will be withdrawing my children from these lessons.

"We entrust our children to teachers in order to provide them with a sound education in traditional subjects, not instruct them on explicit sexual matters, which they can neither cope with physically nor emotionally. With failing standards in reading and writing upon leaving primary school, the government should concentrate on using valuable lesson time on improving the literacy skills of our children."

Mother of three children, West Sussex

7. How the 'safer sex' message is failing our children

Many strategies to improve sexual health are failing because they are promoting contraceptive use by young people as the mark of sexual responsibility without making it clear that every form of contraception has its limitations. While condoms offer some protection against certain STIs, they do not prevent the transmission of all STIs. Research shows that condoms are 85-95 per cent effective in preventing HIV transmission, but they are much less effective in providing protection against other infections, including some of the most common ones such as chlamydia, herpes and human papillomavirus (HPV). The truth is that condoms reduce the risk of acquiring chlamydia from an infected partner by around 50 per cent, and they provide very little protection against HPV which can lead to cervical cancer.[1]

SRE programmes that promote condom use may inadvertently increase the incidence of STIs because the false sense of security given by condoms may lead to more young people becoming sexually active.[2]

As a *Daily Telegraph* leader noted:

> To teach young children that sex is fine so long as it is done safely is like teaching them that it is all right to ride motorcycles at 13, as long as they wear crash-helmets. If as many primary school lessons were devoted to motorcycle riding as to sex education, you can be sure that a great many more children would try it – both with and without crash helmets.[3]

Ignorance is not the problem

Research evidence does not support the common claim that teenage pregnancy rates in the UK are high because young people lack reliable information about contraception and are unable to access it with sufficient

---

[1] Family Education Trust has produced a series of health education leaflets on sexually transmitted infections: *Sexual Spin: Sorting fact from fiction about sexually transmitted infections*, *HPV and You* and *Chlamydia and You*. Sample copies are available upon request.

[2] J Richens, J Imrie, A Copes, 'Condoms and seat belts: the parallels and the lessons', *Lancet* 2000; 355:400-403.

[3] 'The truth about sex', *Daily Telegraph*, 5 April 2002.

ease. A study published in the *British Medical Journal* found that 93 per cent of teenagers who became pregnant had seen a health professional at least once during the previous year and 71 per cent had discussed contraception. The researchers concluded that,

> Teenagers who become pregnant have higher consultation rates than their age matched peers, and most of the difference is owing to consultation for contraception.[4]

Alongside condom advocacy, recent years have seen the vigorous promotion of emergency hormonal birth control (the 'morning-after pill') as a back-up for contraceptive failure or 'unprotected sex'. It was initially believed that the emergency pill would reduce teenage pregnancy and abortion rates. However, an editorial in the *British Medical Journal* cited ten studies worldwide showing that its widespread availability has made no appreciable difference to pregnancy or abortion rates.[5]

If sex education is to show proper respect for young people, it must emphasise that sexual intimacy always has consequences and that no form of contraception can offer guaranteed protection from pregnancy or STIs. Teenagers need to be taught that reproduction is one of the primary functions of sexual intercourse and sex should therefore be set in the context of a faithful, lifelong relationship (i.e. marriage), which provides the most stable environment in which to raise children.[6] Sex education should therefore seek to reinforce the message that young people who are not ready for the responsibilities that come with parenthood should not be engaging in sexual activity.

[4] D Churchill, J Allen, M Pringle, J Hippisley Cox, D Ebdon, M Macpherson et al. 'Consultation patterns and provisions of contraception in general practice before teenage pregnancy', *BMJ*, 2000; 321: 486-489.

[5] A Glasier, 'Emergency Contraception', *BMJ*, 333:560–561.

[6] Patricia Morgan, *Marriage-Lite*, Institute for the Study of Civil Society 2000; Rebecca O'Neill, *Experiments in Living: The Fatherless Family*, Civitas 2002; Harry Benson, *The Conflation of Marriage and Cohabitation in Government Statistics*, Bristol Community Family Trust, 2006.

8. How parents are being squeezed out

A few years ago, after figures were published showing a rise in the number of conceptions to 13-15 year-old girls, Beverley Hughes, the minister for children spoke of the vital role of parents:

> We really need parents to now see themselves as making an absolutely unique and vital contribution to this issue… It is a contribution that I don't think anyone else can actually make.[1]

> We cannot make the deep, sustained progress we want to make, particularly at that vulnerable age group, without fully engaging with parents and getting them on board.[2]

Yet while the government trumpets the importance of parents, it continues to pursue policies that undermine and marginalise them. Perhaps nowhere has the government's true estimation of parents been seen more clearly than in the way they have been excluded from the review of sex education.

Parents excluded from the steering group

In February 2008, when the government launched its review of sex education delivery in schools, parents were conspicuous by their absence on the review body. While there was a very definite emphasis on consultation with young people, with three members of UK Youth Parliament selected to serve on the steering group, no attempt was made to take account of the views of parents, who bear the legal responsibility for the education of their children.

When Family Education Trust asked ministers what opportunities there would be for parents to contribute to the review and what appointments had been made to the steering group to represent parental

[1] *The Guardian*, 26 May 2005.
[2] *ePolitix.com*, 27 May 2005.

views and concerns, we were advised that the steering group would be undertaking a literature review of the evidence that exists on 'whether parents want schools to provide SRE; what topics parents feel should be covered at each key stage; and effective ways of engaging parents'.[3]

Lord Adonis also mentioned that the steering group included a practitioner with 'extensive experience of working with parents to help them talk to their children about sex and relationship issues'.[4] Further enquiries revealed that this was a reference to David Kesterton who heads up the *fpa*'s 'Speakeasy' programme. Given the *fpa*'s view that it is 'paternalistic' to hold that parents are best placed to judge what is in the best interests of their children, we were able to derive no comfort at all from the minister's assurances that an officer of the *fpa* would be representing the views of parents in the review.[5]

Parents' views not sought

Data obtained by Family Education Trust under the Freedom of Information Act reveals that the government-appointed review group on SRE made no attempt to consult parents about what should be taught and when. While the review group sought the views of young people and teachers first-hand, it did not commission any survey of parental concerns.

The Sex Education Forum, in conjunction with the UK Youth Parliament, was commissioned to undertake an online survey to elicit views from young people on what should be covered in SRE at each key stage. This was followed by a two day in-depth consultation with 15 young people looking at how SRE can be improved and 'why young people need SRE'. Similarly, the review group commissioned the Sex Education Forum, in conjunction with the PSHE Subject Association, to conduct an online survey to obtain the views of both primary and secondary school teachers on 'what inhibits better delivery of SRE'.

However, no similar survey was undertaken to seek the views of parents. Instead, the review group invited two of its members to give a presentation based on personal experience and previous research. David Kesterton, the manager of the *fpa*'s 'Speakeasy' programme, was asked

[3] Letter from Lord Adonis, 2 April 2008.
[4] *ibid.*
[5] H Carter, 'Mother no longer knows best, High Court told', *Guardian*, 11 November 2005.

to report on the key issues parents found it difficult to talk to children about, while Professor Roger Ingham from the Centre for Sexual Health Research at the University of Southampton was asked to undertake a review of existing studies of parents' attitudes to school SRE.[6]

The data released under the Freedom of Information Act also revealed that the review group considered five 'options' papers covering the training of teachers, involving outside agencies, providing guidance and support materials, using wider government programmes to improve SRE, and ensuring the involvement of young people in the design of their school's SRE programme. But apart from one brief reference in the paper on guidance and support materials, parents were again conspicuous by their absence.

The government's decision to make PSHE, including SRE, a statutory part of the national curriculum was therefore made without any consultation with parents. In fact the government was intending not to consult on raising the status of PSHE at all. It is only after pressure from Family Education Trust that it finally agreed to ask parents and other members of the general public whether they supported its intention.

Confidential clinics on school premises

Parents are also being undermined by health clinics that are being set up in secondary schools, with a particular emphasis on providing pupils with contraceptive advice and supplies in complete confidence, without the knowledge of their parents. These clinics are known by different names in different parts of the country.

In Oxfordshire schools, children attending a Bodyzone clinic are issued with a welcome form which assures them that 'this is a completely CONFIDENTIAL service...your school/college are not allowed to ask why you are attending Bodyzone' (emphasis in original). The first option on the form is for children to ask for 'The Sexual Health Nurse (for contraception, pregnancy tests, supplies and advice)'. The Bodyzone project pack explains that the family planning nurse can '...issue condoms, emergency contraception and repeat supplies of the pill and injectables without a doctor present'. In schools in many parts of the country,

[6] Professor Ingham is well known for his opposition to any approach that encourages young people to save sex for marriage. He is fully supportive of initiatives that are 'non-judgmental and respectful of confidentiality', believing that young people should not be denied 'the opportunity to form relationships and express their feelings safely in ways they choose to'. *BMJ*, 2000 December 16; 321(7275): 1520–1522.

assistance is offered to girls who wish to obtain an abortion without their parents knowing.

Schools are able to by-pass government guidance on sex and relationships education with its emphasis on parental responsibility and consultation with parents because these projects are operated by health authorities on school premises and not by the school itself. Since Bodyzone and other similar schemes operate outside the school curriculum as a service of the health authority, they are not subject to primary education law or guidance.

In March 2006, the government issued fresh guidance for headteachers, teachers, support staff and governors to help them expand or develop a school nursing service, including the provision of confidential contraceptive and abortion advice to underage pupils. According to the document, *Looking for a School Nurse?* the provision of contraceptive advice, together with 'emergency contraception' and pregnancy testing on school premises, will prevent teenage pregnancies and reduce the rates of sexually transmitted infections.[7]

Alongside the guidance to schools, the government also published the *School Nurse: Practice Development Resource Pack*, offering best practice guidance to school nurses and public health officials. The guidance states that, 'school nurses can raise sexual health and relationship issues with young people and make sure they have access to the kind of information and services they need'. As part of 'best practice', school nurses are encouraged to:

- Provide and promote confidential drop-ins at school and community venues, ensuring they are linked to wider primary health care, family planning and genitourinary medicine (GUM) services. Consider the use of new technologies such as texting or e-mail to improve access.

- Ensure that sex and relationship education [SRE] programmes and services meet the needs of ethnic minority, disabled, bisexual, transgender, gay and lesbian young people. Confront discrimination and challenge prejudice such as homophobia.

- Support young women to access services to make timely choices about emergency contraception, pregnancy or abortion.

[7] Department of Health, *Looking for a School Nurse?* March 2006.

- Clarify the purpose and boundary of your role within SRE, ensure it is clear to young people, use ground rules in sessions and remind young people where they can access confidential support and information.[8]

According to a national mapping survey of on-site sexual health services in secondary and further education settings in England conducted by the Sex Education Forum at the end of 2007, almost 30 per cent of secondary schools are now operating a confidential health clinic with a particular focus on contraception and sexual health.[9]

[8] Department of Health, *School Nurse: Practice Development Resource Pack,* March 2006.

[9] Lucy Emmerson, *National mapping of on-site sexual health services in education settings,* Sex Education Forum and National Children's Bureau, June 2008.

9. Why parents matter

Education law in the UK is clear that parents bear the legal responsibility for the education of their children and that children must be educated in accordance with the wishes of their parents:

> The parent of every child of compulsory school age shall cause him to receive efficient full-time education suitable—
>
> (a) to his age, ability and aptitude, and
>
> (b) to any special educational needs he may have, either by regular attendance at school or otherwise.[1]

> In exercising or performing all their respective powers and duties under the Education Acts, the Secretary of State, local education authorities and the funding authorities shall have regard to the general principle that pupils are to be educated in accordance with the wishes of their parents, so far as that is compatible with the provision of efficient instruction and training and the avoidance of unreasonable public expenditure.[2]

PSHE, and especially SRE, is a particularly sensitive and controversial area. It is therefore important that schools retain discretion and flexibility in order to ensure that parental wishes are respected and that parents remain free to withdraw their children from sex education lessons that they are not happy about. The European Convention on Human Rights states:

> In the exercise of any functions which it assumes in relation to education and to teaching, the State shall respect the right of parents to ensure such education and teaching in conformity with their own religious and philosophical convictions.[3]

The DCSF guidance on Sex and Relationship Education reflects these legal provisions with its strong emphasis on consultation and partnership with parents in the development and review of policies that reflect parents' wishes. The guidance states that it is:

[1] Education Act 1996, s7.
[2] Education Act 1996, s9.
[3] European Convention on Human Rights, First Protocol, Article 2.

essential that governing bodies involve parents in developing and reviewing their policy. This will ensure that they reflect parents' wishes and the culture of the community the school serves.[4]

The guidance goes on to refer to 'the obligation on schools to involve parents in the determination of their sex and relationship education policy',[5] and states that:

> Governors and head teachers should discuss with parents and take on board concerns raised, both on materials which are offered to schools and on sensitive material to be used in the classroom.[6]

We should never lose sight of the fact that the function of schools is to assist parents in fulfilling their legal duty to provide their children with a full-time and efficient education. As servants of parents rather than their lords, it is important that schools should continue to develop their policies in consultation with parents and to be accountable to parents for the education they provide at the local level.

This means that schools will need to develop ways to consult with parents with regard to both their policy on sex and relationship education and its delivery. It is not sufficient to claim that the mere presence of parent-governors on the governing body satisfies their requirement to consult with parents. Rather, schools should have an open attitude towards parents and welcome enquiries about the content and delivery of the PSHE curriculum. Meetings for parents to view the material should be held at a time when most parents will be able to attend, and provision should be made for parents who are unable to attend such a meeting to view the materials at another time. Schools should also be willing to show parents lesson plans and materials used in the delivery of PSHE upon request.

---

[4] Department for Education and Employment, Sex and Relationship Education Guidance, July 2000, Ref 0116/2000, para 1.2.
[5] *ibid.*, para 1.5.
[6] *ibid.*, para 1.8.

10. Should children and young people decide what sex education they receive?

While the importance of consulting with parents and respecting their views is being played down, the government is placing a strong emphasis on listening to young people and is proposing that school governing bodies should be required to consult with them when developing their sex and relationship education policies. When announcing the review of SRE delivery, schools minister Jim Knight stated:

> I am determined that young people be involved in developing this policy. I look forward to working with UK Youth Parliament who have played an important part in bringing this issue to the fore.[1]

According to a survey of 21,602 young people conducted by the UK Youth Parliament, 40 per cent of young people between the ages of 11 and 18 thought that their SRE was either poor or very poor, whilst a further 33 per cent thought it was average. The same survey found that 73 per cent of all respondents felt that SRE should be delivered under the age of 13, with 56 per cent of boys under 11 wanting SRE in primary schools.[2]

In the view of the government, the opinions of young people on sex education are highly significant. On the day after the government launched its review of SRE, the Sex Education Forum launched a government-funded 'toolkit' to help secondary schools canvas young people's opinions on what they think they should learn at various ages. Schools minister Jim Knight said:

> Young people are at the heart of the national review of SRE delivery in schools which we announced yesterday. We are keen to help schools find out whether the SRE they are currently providing to their pupils is meeting their needs, so we have supported the Sex Education Forum to develop the SRE pupil audit

---

[1] Department for Children, Schools and Families, 'Review of Sex and Relationship Education Delivery', Press Notice 2008/0029, 25 February 2008.

[2] UK Youth Parliament, *Are You Getting It?* June 2007.

toolkit. This toolkit will give schools practical ways of involving young people, to ensure they do get the information and support to make safe and healthy choices.[3]

Under the title, *Are you getting it right?* the toolkit contains a series of activities designed to encourage pupils to share their views about what they want to learn in SRE, how they want to learn, and what support and advice they want and need.[4]

Relativism and the subtle undermining of parents

It is evident that the Sex Education Forum is committed to promoting the view that there are no rights and wrongs when it comes to sexual relationships. The activity on a 'moral and values framework' makes it clear that the purpose is 'not to agree the rights and wrongs' of various statements, 'but rather to discover the range of opinions on the subject'. The intention appears to be to steer children away from a belief in moral absolutes and to encourage them to think that everything is relative. The toolkit seems oblivious to the fact that there is a fundamental conflict between the relativistic approach favoured by the Forum and its stated aim of helping young people to make safe and healthy choices. The only truly safe and healthy choice is to follow a clear moral code that keeps sexual intimacy within the context of a faithful and lifelong marriage.

The toolkit is also fundamentally flawed in assuming that children have the maturity and discernment to know what they need in terms of sex and relationships education. No account is taken of the fact that children possess a natural curiosity about some matters that they simply don't need to know about and that it may not be helpful for them to know about. Some things can wait; and there are some sexual practices that it may be better not to know anything about at all, at any age.

The idea that children and young people should have an influence in determining the character of the sex education they receive may sound very reasonable at first glance, but there is a subtle undermining of parental responsibility lurking just below the surface. Whereas government guidance has hitherto placed a strong emphasis on the need for schools to

---

[3] Sex Education Forum press release, 'School pupils will be asked what they want to learn in sex and relationships teaching', 26 February 2008.

[4] Sex Education Forum, *Are you getting it right? A toolkit for consulting young people on sex and relationships education*, February 2008.

consult with parents and to be sensitive to parental wishes since parents are the primary educators and protectors of their children, children are increasingly being treated as autonomous individuals divorced from the supervision of their parents. We are in danger of losing sight of the fact that what children say they want is not necessarily the same as what they need, and it is therefore a serious abdication of adult responsibility to allow the sex education curriculum to be shaped by the views of young people themselves.

Ofsted: Young people's views trump objective facts

The education standards watchdog Ofsted appears to have become so wedded to the idea of listening to the views of young people that objective facts are now taking a second place to letting young people set the policy agenda. In its report on the teaching of PSHE, Ofsted was dismissive of attempts to encourage children to save sex for marriage. The report claimed:

> There is no evidence…that abstinence-only education reduces teenage pregnancy or improves sexual health. There is also no evidence to support claims that teaching about contraception leads to increased sexual activity. Research suggests that education and strategies that promote abstinence but withhold information about contraception can place young people at a higher risk of pregnancy and sexually transmitted infections (STIs).[5]

In subsequent correspondence with Family Education Trust, Ofsted revealed that these claims are based on research published by the Sex Education Forum, which, as we have seen, is a body ideologically opposed to the idea that sex belongs in marriage. However, when we pressed Ofsted on what account they had taken of research showing the success of abstinence education, they said they had not taken any account of it because the report was 'based, in the main, on first-hand evidence from inspectors' visits to schools'.

The Ofsted report also stated that: 'School nurses can…provide a valuable service, particularly in terms of providing emergency hormonal contraception and advising on other forms of contraception.'[6]

---

[5] Ofsted, *Time for change? Personal, social and health education,* April 2007.
[6] *ibid.*

When we asked Ofsted how they could say this when research consistently showed that supplying the morning-after pill was not making the slightest difference to teenage pregnancy and abortion rates, they lamely replied that pupils said they found it useful and helpful. In other words, in the view of the Office for Standards in Education, if pupils value being able to get contraception and the morning-after pill from the school nurse, in strict confidence without Mum and Dad knowing, that makes it a valuable service!

It doesn't bode well for children when the body responsible for evaluating and reporting on the spiritual, moral, social and cultural development of pupils, including commenting on a school's sex and relationship education policy can't tell the difference between what children say they value and what is truly valuable, based on objective evidence.

11. What children and young people really need

Contrary to the prevalent view among sex educators, young people do not need to learn about a wide range of 'sexualities' and sexual behaviours; they do not need detailed information about the full range of contraceptive methods; and they do not need to be presented with a menu of sexual options from which they can make 'informed choices' when they feel they are 'ready' to become sexually active.

Modern sex education is characterised by a lack of honesty, a lack of modesty, a lack of any moral framework worthy of the name, and a lack of respect for marriage as the proper context for sexual expression. Yet it is these missing elements that children and young most need to learn – both by word and by example.

We need to be honest with young people about the consequences of sex

According to the *fpa*, 'ANYONE who has sex can have a sexually transmitted infection'[1] and 'Practising safer sex (using condoms) is the single most important step anyone can take to help prevent getting or spreading STIs.'[2] In response to the question, 'How can I make sure I don't get a sexually transmitted infection?' the *fpa* advises girls that 'condoms give good protection',[3] but fails to mention that keeping sex within a monogamous, faithful marriage to an uninfected spouse offers the best protection of all.

There is a strong resistance among many sex educators towards telling young people about the limitations of condoms to prevent pregnancy and to prevent the transmission of STIs. They reason that if they were to tell young people the truth, they might not use them at all and then they would be at even greater risk. It doesn't seem to occur to them that by concealing the truth and giving the impression that condoms are well-nigh

---

[1] *4 Girls – A Below-the-Bra guide to the female body*, fpa, 2000, emphasis in original.
[2] *Love, Sex and Relationships*, fpa, 2005.
[3] *4 Girls, op. cit.*

100 per cent effective in preventing any unwelcome outcome, they are positively encouraging sexual risk-taking.

The stark reality is that outside of a committed, mutually faithful, lifelong relationship, there is no such thing as 'safe sex'. Young people need to be made aware of the fact that any sexual activity outside the context of a faithful, lifelong, monogamous relationship places them at risk of contracting an STI. True sexual responsibility is marked not by using contraception, but by abstaining from sex outside of a lifelong and faithful relationship, most commonly signified by marriage.

We need to be modest and restrained in how we talk to young people about sex

According to the government, it is never too early for parents to start talking to their children about sex and relationships, and talking openly to teenagers makes them feel under less pressure to have sex.[4] And it is true that some studies have shown that conversations with parents tend to encourage more conservative attitudes, when compared to discussions with peers which often lead to more liberal attitudes.[5] But it is not quite as simple as that, because there have been other studies showing that young people who report having more conversations of a sexual nature with their parents are more likely to become sexually active at an early age.[6]

The evidence indicates that there is no benefit to be gained from engaging in conversations about sex *per se*; what really matters is how it is done. If parents have a casual, blasé approach to sexual issues and allow television programmes and music with high levels of sexual content to be viewed and played in the home, their children are likely to view sexual intimacy as something cheap and to act accordingly. However, if parents speak about sexual matters with modesty and restraint and exercise control over sexual content in the media, then their children will see sexual intimacy as something valuable and worthy of respect.

---

[4] NHS and Parentline Plus, *Talking to your teenager about sex and relationships*.

[5] C DiLorio, M Kelley, M Hockenberry–Eaton, 'Communication about sexual issues: mothers, fathers and friends', *J Adolesc Health* 1999; 24:181–189.

[6] M Bersamin, M Todd, D A Fisher, D L Hill, J W Grube, S Walker, 'Parenting Practices and Adolescent Sexual Behavior: A Longitudinal Study', *Journal of Marriage and Family* 70 (February 2008): 97-112.

We need to give young people clear moral direction

According to a government leaflet drafted by the DCSF and approved by ministers, parents should not teach their children that there are any rights and wrongs when it comes to sex and relationships. The leaflet, *Talking to your teenager about sex and relationships*, tells parents that their children need to know about contraception; sexually transmitted infections; gay, lesbian and bi-sexual teenagers; and alcohol and drugs; but warns parents that teaching their children that anything is right or wrong will be counterproductive. While parents may discuss their 'values' with their teenage children, they are urged to:

> Remember though, that trying to convince them of what's right and wrong may discourage them from being open. Try to keep the discussion light, encourage them to say what they think and reassure them that you trust them to make the right decisions.[7]

There are several references to 'right decisions' and 'right choices', but they are only ever defined in connection with using contraception – what the leaflet inaccurately describes as 'safe sex'. The message communicated is that there is nothing wrong about any kind of sexual relationship in principle, so long as contraception is used. The *fpa*, Brook and Stonewall are recommended as sources of further help and advice, and for 'detailed information on STIs and how to stay protected', parents are encouraged to direct their teenagers to the NHS-funded website *www.condomessentialwear.co.uk* where teenagers are promised: 'This site has all you need to know to keep healthy, stay safe and make condoms a fun and essential part of your sex life.' The leaflet contains not a single mention of marriage, lifelong commitment, or even of love.[8]

In the name of non-judgmentalism, the government's approach is abandoning young people to the shifting sands of relativism and depriving them of the moral compass they so desperately need. As a former US Secretary of Education has noted:

> [Y]ou sometimes get the feeling that, for these guides, being 'comfortable' with one's decision when exercising one's 'option' is the sum and substance of the responsible life. Decisions aren't right or wrong – decisions simply make you

---

[7] *Talking to your teenager about sex and relationships*, op. cit.

[8] *ibid.*

comfortable or not. It is as though 'comfort' alone had now become our moral compass.[9]

Any SRE programme that fails to place sexual intimacy within a clear and objective moral context will inevitably run the risk of encouraging underage sex. This is particularly true if a primary focus of the teaching is on the provision and use of contraception. Advice on how to engage 'safely' in an activity, coupled with provision to facilitate it, conveys the message that the activity itself is acceptable. One study found that 45.5 per cent of boys admitted that when they first received sex education, they felt the need to experiment. Considering that the majority of boys surveyed (77 per cent) had received sex education by the age of 12, this is a particularly disturbing finding.[10]

It is important that pupils are given clear messages about the negative consequences of underage sex and the benefits of saving sex. Sexual intimacy should be seen not in terms of personal gratification, but as an adult expression of love and commitment between lifelong partners in marriage. Placing sexual activity within this framework will not only encourage teenagers to refrain from sex and resist peer pressure, but it will also satisfy the legal requirement placed on schools to provide sex education 'in such a manner as to encourage... pupils to have due regard to moral considerations and the value of family life'.[11]

What young people really need is not more talk about the mechanics of sex and contraception, but encouragement to develop the character qualities of stability, faithfulness and commitment - the qualities they will need in order to build a strong and lasting marriage based on something that runs deeper than feelings and physical attraction. And that is done primarily by example. Given the misery that so often flows from casual relationships, the best advice parents can give their children is to avoid forming an exclusive friendship with someone from the opposite sex until they are in a position to seriously consider getting married.

[9] William Bennett, 'Sex and the Education of our Children', an address delivered at a meeting of the National School Boards Association in January 1987.
[10] Royal Forest of Dean College with Gloucestershire Community Health Council, *Sex Education & Family Planning Services Survey Results*, March 2000.
[11] Education Act 1996, s403(1).

We need to stress the positive benefits of saving sex for marriage

In view of the health risks associated with underage sex and the high levels of regret associated with early sexual activity,[12] there is a strong case for actively discouraging sexual experimentation and showing the positive benefits of reserving sex for a lifelong and faithful marriage where it serves as an expression of the total self-giving of a husband and wife to each other.

All too often teaching aimed at encouraging young people to refrain from sexual intimacy outside the marriage bond is portrayed in a negative way and dismissed as a matter of 'just saying no'. In reality, however, there is much more to it than that. It involves understanding the true meaning and purpose of sex and leads to freedom from fear, embarrassment, shame and emotional pain, as well as freedom from physical disease.

To present young people with the positive reasons for saving sexual intimacy until they commit themselves to a person of the opposite sex for life is to help them to lay foundations that will lead to a more trusting marriage. The joys and benefits of saving sex for a healthy, trusting, committed marriage far outweigh any passing pleasure gained from early sexual experimentation.[13]

[12] K Wellings et al, 'Sexual Health in Britain: early heterosexual experience', *Lancet*, 2001, vol.358:1834-1850.

[13] Family Education Trust has produced a leaflet for young people setting out positive reasons for saving sex for marriage. Entitled *Why Save Sex?* it has been welcomed by schools and youth settings throughout the UK. Sample copies are available on request.

Conclusion

The teenage pregnancy strategy is clearly not working and there is widespread agreement that the government has no realistic hope of achieving its target by 2010. In addition, STI rates have risen dramatically, and there has been a marked increase in the percentage of teenage pregnancies ended by abortion.

The teenage pregnancy strategy has sent out two particularly damaging messages to children and young people:

- There is nothing wrong with sex at any age, and
- Whether you have sex has got nothing to do with your parents.

Over recent years we have witnessed the systematic removal of every restraint which in previous generations served as a disincentive to underage sexual activity:

- sex education in many schools has had the effect of breaking down the natural inhibitions of children with regard to sexual conduct;
- the age of consent is rarely enforced, so young people no longer have any fear of legal proceedings;
- the ready availability of contraception means that a girl's fear of pregnancy is no longer considered a good enough reason for rejecting her boyfriend's advances; and
- confidentiality policies mean that a girl need not worry about what her parents would think about her being sexually active, obtaining contraception, being treated for an STI or even having an abortion, because they need not know.

So what should be done?

There is no quick fix, but the government's reliance on earlier sex education and more contraception is misplaced and is proving counterproductive. The idea that making PSHE statutory from the very beginning of primary school is going to have a positive impact is little more than wishful thinking.

- There is a lack of evidence for the effectiveness of PSHE, or even agreement as to what constitutes effectiveness;
- The push for statutory PSHE has been driven by a sex education lobby that has a vested financial interest and the government has capitulated to a concerted and well-orchestrated campaign;
- To make PSHE statutory would inevitably reduce the influence of parents over what is taught and remove discretion from parents and schools at the local level.

What we really need is to recover a proper respect for marriage and a proper respect for parents.

Respect for marriage

Sex has become so cheapened in a world obsessed with sexual expression that we have lost sight of its special character. Often it is seen merely as a casual, recreational activity to bring personal pleasure. But sex is not intended to be just about the joining of two bodies together, but the joining of two lives. In the context of faithful, lifelong marriage, sexual intimacy expresses the total self-giving of a husband and wife to each other.

Separating sex from marriage has not only led to high rates of teenage pregnancy, sexually transmitted infection and abortion, but it is also a major contributory factor in divorce and family breakdown and all the human misery and adverse social consequences that flow from it. It is therefore important that sexual intimacy should always be spoken of within a clear moral context, that the consequences of sexual activity are honestly faced and that the positive benefits of saving sexual intimacy for marriage are clearly presented.

Respect for parents

It is vital that schools remain accountable to parents for the sex education they provide and that parents are fully involved in the development of the school's policy. Where parents are unable to reach agreement with the school with regard to the delivery of sex education, it is important that they retain the right to withdraw their children from classes.

There also needs to be a reversal of policies that allow secondary school pupils to receive advice on contraception and access to contraceptive and abortion services on school premises without the knowledge of their parents. A proper respect for parents means encouraging them to take responsibility for their children, not undermining them and excluding them from their children's lives.

For further reading

Books

HIV and Aids in Schools: The political economy of pressure groups and miseducation
Barrie Craven, Pauline Dixon, Gordon Stewart and James Tooley, IEA, 2001.

Hooked: New science on how casual sex is affecting our children
Joe S McIlhaney and Freda McKissic Bush, Northfield Publishing, 2008.

Questions kids ask about sex: Honest answers for every age
J Thomas Fitch and Melissa R Cox (eds), Revell, 2005.

Sex Education or Indoctrination? How ideology has triumphed over facts
Valerie Riches, Family Education Trust, 2004.

Sex Under Sixteen? Young people comment on the social and educational influences on their behaviour
Clifford Hill, Family Education Trust, 2000.

Waking Up to the Morning-After Pill: How parents are being undermined by the promotion of emergency hormonal birth control to under-16s
Norman Wells and Helena Hayward, Family Education Trust, 2007.

Leaflets

Chlamydia and You

HPV and You

Respect Begins at Home: Why the government needs to show parents more respect

Sexual Spin: Sorting fact from fiction about sexually transmitted infections

Why Save Sex?

All the above titles are available from Family Education Trust, Jubilee House, 19-21 High Street, Whitton, Twickenham TW2 7LB email: info@famyouth.org.uk website: www.famyouth.org.uk

Deconstructing the Dutch Utopia: Sex education and teenage pregnancy in the Netherlands by Joost van Loon is now out of print, but can be downloaded free of charge from the Family Education Trust website at http://www.famyouth.org.uk/issues.php?pagename=DDUinfo